FINANCIAL FREEDOM PLANNING

Your Comprehensive Blueprint to Achieve Financial Freedom Through Strategic Planning, Smart Money Management, and a Lifetime of Wealth Building Strategies"

Michael J. Ferrell

Table of contents

INTRODUCTION

With just one handbook in hand, Sarah set out on her mission to achieve financial independence amid a busy metropolis. The title of the guide was "Financial Freedom Planning." Following the detailed plan that was presented in the book, she did so with a strong sense of resolve serving as her compass. Throughout her whole life, Sarah has painstakingly carried out a series of wealth-building methods using strategic planning and intelligent money management.

When she was confronted with financial difficulties, she accepted the principles of the book and created a budget that was in line with her objectives. The investments that Sarah made were varied, and she took cautious risks while also capitalizing on opportunities. Throughout her journey, the book's sage advice helped her weather the storms of the economy, so assuring her that she would have a financially stable future.

The systematic approach that Sarah took to the ideas that were detailed in "Financial Freedom Planning" completely altered the geography of her financial situation. Through the years, she was able to accomplish milestones that had previously seemed to be unachievable, all while planting the seeds for future generations to be wealthy. Her accomplishments served as a demonstration of the transformational potential of the all-encompassing blueprint, demonstrating that achieving financial independence was not only a pipe dream but rather an attainable reality via the application of devotion and strategic preparation.

Sarah was able to find her way to financial independence by following the intelligent advice provided by "Financial Freedom Planning" when she was in the middle of the hustle and bustle of the city. The book, with its elaborate subtitle offering a full strategy for success, became her lighthouse amid the jungle of economic difficulties.

Sarah's adventure started as she absorbed the book's lessons on strategic planning, savvy money management, and a lifetime of wealth-building tactics. Armed with this information, she methodically established a budget that served as the cornerstone for her financial pursuits. Each cost was analyzed, and every dollar found significance in the pursuit of her long-term objectives.

The thorough plan presented in the book became Sarah's roadmap, bringing her through the twists and turns of the financial environment. It challenged her to diversify her assets, training her to discriminate between risk and opportunity. In times of economic instability, the knowledge hidden in the pages of "Financial Freedom Planning" provided a stable anchor, guiding her actions and sheltering her from possible dangers.

As the years unfolded, Sarah's diligent approach produced results. Her investments grew, and her financial fortune increased. The book's concepts were not only theoretical; they were the building blocks of her success. The subtitle's promise of a lifetime of wealth-building tactics held as Sarah built not simply monetary riches but a legacy of financial stability.

Sarah's tale became a witness to the transformational power of strategic planning and wise money management. The book that previously appeared as a modest guide has become the cornerstone of her financial freedom. Through devotion and attention to the ideas established in "Financial Freedom Planning," Sarah converted the ideal of financial independence into a realistic reality, leaving a lasting legacy for generations to come.

Embarking on a road toward financial independence involves more than simply a desire for riches; it demands a full comprehension of essential ideas and a planned strategy. In this series, we look into important components that create the core of financial success. From setting the scene for your financial future to the subtleties of strategic planning, each chapter is intended to provide you with the information and skills required to navigate the complicated world of personal finance.

Setting the Stage for Financial Freedom

In the quest for financial independence, building a firm foundation is crucial. This requires not just analyzing your present financial situation but also projecting your desired future. Begin by making a detailed review of your income, spending, assets, and obligations. Identify areas for development and create clear financial objectives. Whether it's creating an emergency fund, reducing debt, or investing for long-term development, a well-defined path is vital.

Furthermore, having an attitude of financial discipline is crucial. This entails making educated judgments about spending, saving, and investing. Consider creating sustainable behaviors that coincide with your financial goals. Cultivate the discipline to discriminate between necessities and desires, making intentional decisions that contribute to your overall financial well-being.

Moreover, examining numerous revenue options might strengthen your financial security. While a main career may give a stable income, diversifying via side hustles or investments may provide alternative opportunities for wealth building. Setting the scene for financial independence is not a one-size-fits-all undertaking; customize your strategy to correspond with your circumstances and ambitions.

The Importance of Strategic Planning

Strategic planning acts as the compass directing your financial path. It comprises a detailed review of your present financial status and the design of a path that corresponds with your goals. Consider your short-term and long-term objectives, risk tolerance, and time horizon. Crafting a well-thought-out financial strategy helps you to make educated choices and overcome uncertainty.

One key part of strategic planning is budgeting. Establishing a realistic budget ensures that your money is spent properly, meeting needed costs while allowing for savings and investments. Regularly examine and revise your budget as circumstances change, maintaining a dynamic strategy that adjusts to life's increasing needs.

Investment strategy is another cornerstone of strategic planning. Diversifying your investing portfolio across several asset types helps decrease risk and boost possible rewards. Whether it's stocks, bonds, real estate, or other investment vehicles, a diversified strategy may weather market swings and contribute to long-term financial success.

Additionally, evaluate the necessity of risk management within your strategy plan. Life is unpredictable, and unanticipated circumstances might damage your financial stability. Incorporate insurance plans and emergency cash into your strategy to offset unexpected setbacks, ensuring that you have a safety net in place.

In conclusion, setting the scene for financial independence and adopting strategic planning are key components of a successful financial journey. By building a disciplined mentality, diversifying income sources, and creating a well-thought-out strategic plan, you empower yourself to manage the complexity of personal finance and begin on a road toward enduring financial success.

Chapter 1:

Understanding Your Financial Landscape

In the complicated tapestry of personal finance, getting a comprehensive awareness of your financial environment is the beginning leap toward constructing a safe and wealthy future. This chapter goes into the key parts of knowing your financial situation, setting realistic objectives, and resolving frequent obstacles that may impair your financial well-being.

Assessing present Financial Health Begin your road to financial empowerment by taking a comprehensive evaluation of your present financial health. This entails analyzing revenue sources, monitoring spending, and appraising current assets and obligations. By studying these components, you may find significant insights about your financial situation, helping you to make educated choices and develop a healthy foundation for your future ventures.

Identifying Aspirations and Goals

Aspirations and objectives act as the compass directing your financial path. This part fosters reflection, asking you to outline your short-term and long-term ambitions. Whether it's acquiring a house, supporting college, or investing for retirement, identifying your objectives is crucial in establishing a personalized financial strategy. This chapter includes tools and insights to help you express and prioritize your ambitions, matching them with your specific financial environment.

Addressing Common Financial Pain Points

Financial issues are an inevitable part of life, but identifying and tackling them head-on may lessen their effect. This part navigates through typical financial pain areas, presenting real answers and techniques to overcome them. Whether battling with debt, inadequate funds, or investing issues, this chapter offers you the information to design successful treatments. By identifying and resolving these difficulties, you may pave the road to financial resilience and stability.

Embrace this chapter as a blueprint to navigate the twists and turns of your financial terrain. As you engage on this road, remember that financial literacy is an ongoing process. By evaluating your present financial health, making meaningful objectives, and facing difficulties, you create the framework for a safe and profitable financial future.

Chapter 2: Smart Money Management

Budgeting Techniques for Sustainable Living

In the domain of personal money, understanding the skill of budgeting is crucial for attaining sustainable living. A well-crafted budget serves as the cornerstone of financial stability, helping people to manage resources prudently and make educated financial choices.

Budgeting Essentials

Begin by analyzing your income and classifying expenses. Adopt a zero-based budgeting strategy, ensuring every dollar has a purpose. Allocate monies to needs like housing, utilities, and food while allowing enough for discretionary spending and savings.

Technology Integration: Leverage technology to simplify budgeting. Numerous applications give real-time insights into spending habits, allowing for modifications as required. Automation solutions may simplify bill payments and savings contributions, lowering the chance of oversights.

Sustainable Practices: Incorporate sustainable practices into your budget. Consider the environmental effect of your purchasing, selecting eco-friendly items and energy-efficient alternatives. Aligning financial choices with environmental conscience promotes a holistic approach to sustainable living.

Debt Management Strategies

Debt, when handled wisely, becomes a tool for financial success rather than a burden. This chapter digs into efficient debt management tactics, offering light on approaches to decrease debt and establish a healthy financial future.

Debt Prioritization: Identify and prioritize high-interest obligations. Develop a repayment plan that focuses on clearing debts with the highest interest rates first, gradually moving towards those with lower rates. This technique decreases interest accrual, speeding the route to debt independence.

Consolidation Options:

Explore debt consolidation as a potential approach. Combining various loans into a single, manageable loan with a reduced interest rate may simplify payments and decrease total interest expenses. However, rigorous study is necessary to locate credible consolidation choices.

Financial Counseling: Consider getting professional financial counseling if debt becomes unbearable. Certified credit counselors may give specialized help, aiding in setting realistic repayment schedules and negotiating with creditors.

Building Emergency Funds and Safety Nets

Financial stability rests on the capacity to handle unanticipated occurrences. This chapter stresses the significance of having solid emergency accounts and safety nets to defend against unforeseen financial shocks.

Emergency Fund Basics:

Establishing an emergency fund is a cornerstone of financial resiliency. Aim to collect three to six months' worth of living costs in a designated savings account. This fund functions as a financial buffer, delivering peace of mind and security during times of uncertainty.

Insurance Considerations

Incorporate insurance as a critical component of your safety net. Ensure enough coverage for health, property, and income protection. Understanding insurance specifics and frequently reassessing coverage levels assures that your safety net stays sturdy and matched with shifting demands.

Investment Diversification: Explore numerous investment possibilities to improve your financial safety net. Diversification across asset types mitigates risks and boosts overall portfolio resilience. Consult with a financial adviser to personalize investing strategies to your unique risk tolerance and financial objectives.

Chapter 3: Investment Fundamentals for Long-Term Growth

In the quest of financial success, knowing investing principles is crucial. Successful wealth-building depends on a strong foundation, and this chapter digs into the main ideas that support long-term development. From grasping risk and return dynamics to navigating market trends, we untangle the complexity of investing, offering a blueprint for those seeking sustainable financial progress.

The cornerstone of this chapter is in understanding the notion of compound interest, a potent force that may enormously multiply wealth over time. We analyze numerous investing vehicles, ranging from equities and bonds to mutual funds and retirement accounts, giving insights into their unique risk profiles and possible returns. By establishing a complete awareness of investing basics, readers are empowered to make educated choices that match with their financial objectives.

Real Estate Strategies for Wealth Accumulation

Real estate stands as a lasting path for wealth building, and this chapter digs into the tactics that might make property ownership into a prosperous endeavor. From residential homes to commercial endeavors, we explore the complexity of real estate investing, leading readers through the subtleties of property selection, financing, and management.

Examining the cyclical nature of real estate markets, we identify chances for smart entry and exit points, enabling investors to benefit from market swings. Tax ramifications, financing choices, and property management best practices are explained to equip readers with the information required to negotiate the evolving environment of real estate investing. Whether striving for rental income, property appreciation, or both, this chapter presents a complete approach to leveraging real estate as a cornerstone of wealth-building.

Diversification and Risk Mitigation

In the uncertain world of finance, diversity arises as a buffer against volatility, and risk mitigation

Chapter 4: Lifetime Wealth Strategies

Retirement Planning and Long-Term Security

In the ever-evolving environment of financial planning, establishing a pleasant retirement serves as a cornerstone. As we dig into the subtleties of retirement planning, we traverse the difficulties of investment portfolios, risk management, and the ever-elusive goal of financial independence.

Retirement planning is not a one-size-fits-all undertaking. Each individual's path is unique, necessitating a specialized approach. From 401(k)s to IRAs, the route to retirement takes savvy decision-making and forethought. Diversification becomes a crucial factor, minimizing risk and ensuring that your nest egg weathers market changes.

Long-term security is not only about generating money; it's about conserving it. Intelligent investing techniques paired with frequent reassessments are crucial. As we investigate the paths of annuities, bonds, and stocks, we find the instruments that shelter our financial fortresses from the storms of economic unpredictability.

Legacy Planning and Wealth Transfer

Beyond one's lifetime, the legacy persists. Legacy planning exceeds just cash bequests; it involves principles, knowledge, and a design for the generations that follow. It's about generating a lasting impression that reverberates across time.

Wealth transfer tactics become essential in this goal. Trusts, wills, and giving mechanisms take center stage as we uncover the subtleties of passing on riches. Careful care is given to tax considerations, ensuring that the wealth transfer is not encumbered by unwanted encumbrances.

However, legacy planning is not bound to numbers and regulations. It's about conveying a narrative—crafting a tale that mirrors your ideals and objectives. We dig into the art of generosity, examining ways where your riches might contribute to causes that connect with your beliefs, creating a legacy that stretches well beyond financial holdings.

Maximizing Financial Efficiency

In the maze of personal finance, efficiency is the compass that directs us to ideal results. Maximizing financial efficiency is not only about decreasing costs; it's a comprehensive strategy that balances revenue, spending, and investments.

Strategic budgeting takes priority as we analyze spending patterns, ensuring resources are used carefully. Tax efficiency becomes a key, investigating deductions, credits, and exemptions to reduce the tax burden. Moreover, strategic debt management is explored, discriminating between "good" and "bad" debt, and leveraging credit properly.

The efficient deployment of assets is a main focus. Whether it's managing investment portfolios or examining the performance of financial instruments, the objective is to generate the maximum returns with the least risk. Through this perspective, we negotiate the nuances of financial markets, asset allocation, and the quest for optimum returns.

Chapter 5: Financial Considerations for Entrepreneurs

Navigating Career and Entrepreneurial Paths

In today's changing professional world, understanding the skill of navigating career and entrepreneurial routes is important for sustainable success. This chapter digs into crucial areas, including insights into financial concerns for entrepreneurs, maximizing career transitions, and developing numerous sources of income.

Launching into the enterprise is a thrilling trip, but financial prudence is the compass that leads lasting success. Entrepreneurs must rigorously plan and manage their money to weather uncertainty and capitalize on opportunities. From planning and resource allocation to comprehending cash flow dynamics, this section gives a thorough approach to financial savvy in the business sphere. Real-world case studies and expert insights reveal the subtleties of financial decision-making, helping entrepreneurs to establish resilient companies that survive the test of time.

Optimizing Career Transitions

Career changes are unavoidable in a continuously developing employment environment. Whether navigating a promotion, transferring sectors, or accepting a new job, strategic preparation is crucial. This section digs into practical tactics for improving job transitions, from sharpening transferable abilities to establishing a compelling personal brand. Readers will study the psychology of change, learn to harness networking opportunities, and get practical strategies to handle the challenges of professional growth. Expert advice and success stories give inspiration and insight, ensuring that each shift becomes a stepping stone toward greater career satisfaction.

Creating Multiple Streams of Income Diversification is the cornerstone of financial stability. In an age when flexibility is crucial, generating numerous sources of income is an effective approach for both professionals and entrepreneurs. This section unpacks the notion of income diversification, investigating alternatives such as investments, side hustles, and passive income sources. Practical recommendations on risk management and growing revenue streams equip readers with a path to financial stability. Insightful conversations with people who have effectively diversified their income sources provide vital insights and urge readers to begin their paths toward financial freedom.

As the reader goes through this chapter, a complete picture of career and entrepreneurial navigation develops. From the complexity of financial management to the art of smooth job changes and the empowerment that comes with generating several revenue streams, this chapter offers people the information and skills required to survive in today's changing professional environment.

In conclusion, mastering the chapters of one's professional path takes a diverse approach. By accepting the ideas mentioned in this chapter, people may negotiate the difficulties of professional and entrepreneurial routes with confidence, resilience, and a strategic mentality. As the adage goes, success favors the prepared, and this chapter serves as a guide for individuals equipped to explore and conquer the many terrains of their professional destiny.

Chapter 6: Overcoming Common Challenges

In the quest for financial success, people typically meet a multiplicity of problems that reach beyond the domain of statistics and spreadsheets. Chapter 6 dives into the psychological hurdles that might obstruct one's financial path, the flexibility necessary to negotiate economic shifts, and the transforming potential of converting setbacks into opportunities.

Psychological Barriers to Financial Success

Achieving financial success is not only about statistics; it is also a psychological journey. This section addresses the delicate relationship between thinking and financial well-being. Probing the depths of typical psychological obstacles such as fear, self-doubt, and procrastination, readers will acquire insights into how these hurdles might be conquered.

By understanding the psychology underlying financial choices, people may build techniques to reduce impulsive tendencies and encourage a disciplined approach to money management. Whether it's tackling the fear of investing or breaking free from limiting ideas, this chapter encourages readers to create a resilient attitude required for long-term financial success.

Adapting to Economic Changes

The financial environment is dynamic and susceptible to frequent adjustments and economic swings. Adapting to these developments is vital for keeping and strengthening one's financial situation. This section includes a detailed analysis of economic changes and their influence on personal finances.

From handling inflationary pressures to capitalizing on new opportunities, readers will receive practical insights on developing a robust financial strategy. The chapter stresses the necessity of diversification, risk management, and remaining educated to not only weather economic storms but also prosper under uncertainty.

Turning Setbacks into Opportunities

Setbacks are unavoidable in any financial path. However, it is the capacity to convert these setbacks into opportunities that divides those who just survive from those who flourish. This section discusses the art of resilience and the strategic method to come back stronger following financial losses.

Readers will be taken through real-life instances of people who transformed financial hardships into stepping stones for achievement. Whether confronting job loss, market downturns, or unanticipated bills, the answer lies in developing a proactive mentality and harnessing setbacks as drivers for personal and financial progress.

Chapter 7: Achieving permanent financial freedom

In the search for financial independence, Chapter 7 serves as the capstone of your journey, concentrating on crucial components that assure permanent success. From monitoring and changing your financial plan to celebrating milestones and triumphs, this chapter gives a complete guide to not just gaining financial independence but also keeping it.

Monitoring and Adjusting Your Financial Plan

Sustainable financial independence involves a diligent attitude to reviewing and updating your financial strategy. Regularly assessing your budget, investments, and financial objectives is vital for reacting to changing circumstances. Embrace a proactive approach, finding areas for improvement and making educated modifications to keep on target.

As you evaluate your financial plan, consider issues such as income variations, unanticipated spending, and market movements. Embrace flexibility, knowing that a dynamic strategy helps you to negotiate the ever-evolving environment of personal finance. By being educated and responsive, you position yourself to overcome difficulties and embrace new chances.

Celebrating Milestones and Successes

Amidst the search for financial freedom, it's crucial to identify and enjoy the milestones and victories along the route. Whether it's paying off a major debt, attaining a savings target, or obtaining a handsome investment return, these achievements deserve acknowledgment.

Celebrating milestones not only delivers a feeling of achievement but also encourages excellent financial habits. Create a process for appreciating triumphs, whether it's a modest personal treat or sharing your success with friends and family.

Cultivate thankfulness for success accomplished, generating a positive mentality that inspires continuous attention to your financial objectives.

Inspiring Others: Building a Community of Financial Freedom Seekers

True financial independence goes beyond personal success—it entails empowering others to begin on their paths toward financial well-being. Building a community of like-minded people fosters a supportive atmosphere where experiences and information may be exchanged, supporting collective progress.

Share your financial success stories, lessons gained, and techniques implemented to inspire and advise others. Establishing a community of financial freedom searchers generates a network of support, incentives, and accountability. As you contribute to the success of others, you reaffirm your dedication to your financial path, creating a positive circle of inspiration and accomplishment.

Chapter 7 contains the core of gaining and maintaining sustainable financial independence. By continuously reviewing and updating your financial plan, celebrating successes, and motivating others, you not only consolidate your success but also contribute to the greater movement of persons pursuing financial independence. Embrace the constant development of your financial path, realizing that genuine freedom is a continuous process of growth, adaptation, and shared achievement.

CONCLUSION

The Journey Ahead: Sustaining Financial Freedom

In today's volatile economic world, obtaining financial independence is a milestone, but keeping it is a journey that takes continual dedication and smart preparation. As we continue on the journey to enduring financial independence, it becomes vital to dive into fundamental ideas and habits that contribute to a solid financial future.

Embracing Financial Literacy

A vital component of retaining financial independence is having a solid grasp of financial literacy. Educating oneself about budgeting, investment techniques, and debt management creates a good basis for making educated financial choices. This empowerment is not a one-time activity but a continuing commitment to keeping educated about market trends, economic developments, and developing financial products.

Cultivating a Savings Mindset

Savings are the cornerstone of financial stability. Beyond the initial gain of money, keeping financial independence entails establishing a disciplined savings attitude. Regular contributions to emergency funds, retirement accounts, and long-term savings vehicles contribute to a financial safety net, providing resilience in the event of unanticipated circumstances.

Diversification and Risk Management

An important element in wealth sustainability is the wise control of risks via diversification. Building a broad investment portfolio that encompasses several asset classes helps lessen the effect of market volatility. Periodic assessments and modifications ensure that the portfolio matches with evolving financial objectives and risk tolerance levels.

Adaptive Financial Planning

The route to sustainable financial independence involves adaptive financial planning. Life is unpredictable, and financial objectives may vary over time. Regularly reassessing financial goals and changing them to fit life changes ensures that the route to financial independence stays relevant and successful. Flexibility in financial planning is a critical aspect of managing the ever-changing economic environment.

Smart Money Management for Generations

Encouraging a Lifetime Commitment to Smart Money Management and Wealth Building

As we seek financial independence, it is not just about safeguarding our future but also about encouraging a dedication to prudent money management throughout generations. Teaching financial literacy to children and successors becomes a legacy that transcends individual successes.

Education as the Foundation

Instilling a lifelong commitment to good money management starts with education. Teaching youngsters about the value of money, the principles of budgeting, and the need to save lays a foundation for healthy financial habits. This early exposure produces a solid financial attitude that may steer them through many life phases.

Leading by Example

Parents and mentors have a key influence in shaping financial practices. Leading by example means exhibiting appropriate money management, making smart financial choices, and showcasing the advantages of long-term planning. This hands-on approach instills a feeling of financial responsibility that persists over a lifetime.

Collaborative Wealth Building

Encouraging a lifelong commitment to wise money management is not a single task. Collaborative wealth development entails working together as a family unit to create financial objectives, manage resources prudently, and celebrate common successes. This collaborative approach develops a feeling of shared responsibility and improves the financial fabric of the family.

Legacy Planning for Future Generations

Sustaining financial independence is not just about personal accomplishment but also about building a lasting legacy for future generations. Implementing proper estate planning allows the seamless transfer of wealth, reducing tax effects and creating a sound financial basis for successors. This forward-thinking strategy sustains the cycle of prudent money Management.

In conclusion, the route ahead toward preserving financial independence is diverse. It needs a commitment to constant learning, a disciplined savings attitude, cautious risk management, and adaptable financial planning. Encouraging a lifelong commitment to sensible money management not only guarantees our financial well-being but also builds a legacy that extends to future generations. As we traverse the complexity of the financial world, let us aim for a healthy balance between personal financial achievement and the empowerment of those who will follow in our footsteps.

www.ingramcontent.com/pod-product-compliance
Lightning Source LLC
Chambersburg PA
CBHW070217260726
48658CB00006BA/2102